Sandra Deneke, Inga Ettelt, Karin Möcklinghoff, Kevin Marc Patterson

Herausgeberin: Sandra Deneke

Englisch 5/6

1. Auflage, 2. korrigierter Nachdruck 2010

Bestellnummer 61277

Diese Zeichen findest du in diesem Buch

Diese Zeichen bei den Aufgaben sagen dir, was du tun könntest:

 Hört das Tonbeispiel an

 Schreibe in dein Heft

 Arbeite mit einem Partner oder einer Partnerin

 Beschaffe dir Informationen

 Hier hilft dir die Grammatik-Seite weiter

 Achtung! Hier musst du aufpassen

Diese Zeichen am unteren Rand sagen dir etwas zum Lernbereich:

Hören und Verstehen
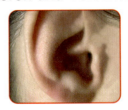

Sprechen
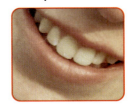

Schreiben

Mit Texten arbeiten

Wortschatz erweitern
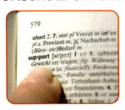

Mit Sprache richtig umgehen

www.bildungsverlag1.de

Bildungsverlag EINS GmbH
Sieglarer Straße 2, 53842 Troisdorf

ISBN 978-3-427-**61277**-3

© Copyright 2008: Bildungsverlag EINS GmbH, Troisdorf
Das Werk und seine Teile sind urheberrechtlich geschützt. Jede Nutzung in anderen als den gesetzlich zugelassenen Fällen bedarf der vorherigen schriftlichen Einwilligung des Verlages.
Hinweis zu § 52a UrhG: Weder das Werk noch seine Teile dürfen ohne eine solche Einwilligung eingescannt und in ein Netzwerk eingestellt werden. Dies gilt auch für Intranets von Schulen und sonstigen Bildungseinrichtungen.

Contents

1 **Welcome to English:
I can speak English** 6
   Denglisch 8   englische Begriffe erkennen
   At the supermarket 9   englische Begriffe erkennen
   English around the world 10   sich über die Weltsprache Englisch austauschen
   The pupils from my class 11   die Herkunft der Mitschüler erfragen

2 **About me: You and I** 12
   Rock around the clock 14   Zahlen von 1 bis 12 kennenlernen
   Hello 15   sich vorstellen
   Meeting friends 16   sich bekannt machen, jemanden vorstellen
   This is me 18   Auskunft erteilen
   Strategy: How to make word cards 20
   This is what you have learned 21

3 **At school: Our classroom** 22
   The colour of the classroom 24   Vorlieben ausdrücken
   Renovation week 25   Wochentage
   A riddle 26   Schule
   Schoolthings-chant 27   Besitzverhältnisse ausdrücken
   I see a girl 28   Farben
   Everything is gone! 29   Auskunft erteilen
   Strategy: Well organised? 30
   This is what you have learned 31

4 **Free time:
Sports and hobbies** 32
   What about you-rap 34   Vorlieben ausdrücken
   What are their hobbies? 35   Aktivitäten beschreiben
   Interview about hobbies 36   Vorlieben/Abneigungen ausdrücken
   Strategy: How to do an interview 38
   A class interview 39   Informationen über Hobbys einholen
   This is what you have learned 40

Contents

5 My body: Descriptions 42
At the mirror cabinet	44	sich selbst und andere beschreiben
A new page in your me-book!	45	sich selbst und andere beschreiben
Who is who?	46	Beschreibungen verstehen und zuordnen
Parts of the body	47	Körperteile
Alien	48	Personen beschreiben
Alien gallery	49	Körperteile benennen
Strategy: Tell your class	50	
This is what you have learned	51	

6 Pets and animals: Our pets 52
My pet	54	Tiere beschreiben
More pets	55	Tiere beschreiben
Pet interview	56	Fragen einüben
What Paul and Emily found out	57	Auskunft erteilen
Strategy: Our animal exhibition	58	
This is what you have learned	60	

7 Around the house: At home .. 62
How people live	64	Gegenstände beschreiben
Paul's new home	65	Gegenstände beschreiben
Moving house	66	Möbel
The new house	67	Haus
A designing project	68	Vorlieben ausdrücken
Strategy: Writing an e-mail	69	
Paul will live somewhere new	70	sich über Zukünftiges austauschen
This is what you have learned	71	

8 Around town: Going places .. 72
What is where?	74	sich nach dem Standort erkundigen/ Fragestruktur mit „Where …?"/ Wortschatzerweiterung
Out and about in the city	76	Auskunft erteilen

Strategy: Reading a map 77
Means of transportation 78
Looking for the music shop 80
This is what you have learned 81

mit dem Wörterbuch arbeiten

Einen Text inhaltlich erfassen können

9 Around the world: Education in Great Britain ... 82

School in Great Britain 84
Designing a new school uniform 85
A visit from Clara 86
This is my day 87
Paul's timetable 88
Strategy: Pros and cons 89
School uniforms 90
This is what you have learned 91

Informationen austauschen
Arbeitsergebnisse vorstellen
einen Sachverhalt beschreiben
Erfassen der Uhrzeit
sich über Vorlieben/Abneigungen austauschen

einen Sachtext verstehen

10 Around the year: Halloween, Christmas, Easter 92

Witch, witch come to my party! 94
Halloween night 96
About Halloween 97
Celebrating Christmas 98
Christmas in Great Britain 99
Jingle Bells 100
Christmas in other countries 101
Celebrating Christmas 102
The cress eggs 103

Geschichten verstehen
einen Reim auswendig lernen
landeskundliche Informationen lesen
seine Meinung äußern
Arbeitsanweisungen befolgen
ein Lied hören und singen
Traditionen miteinander vergleichen
Ortsangaben machen
Handlungsanweisungen verstehen und umsetzen

11 Grammar: To play with language 104

Grammar: Summary 114
Dictionary 126
In English, please! 134

1 Welcome to English:

I can speak English

1 Welcome to English:

Denglisch

Oh Herr, bitte gib mir meine Sprache zurück,
ich sehne mich nach Frieden und 'nem kleinen Stückchen Glück.
Lass uns noch ein Wort verstehn in dieser schweren Zeit,
öffne unsre Herzen, mach' die Hirne weit.

Du versuchst, mich upzudaten, doch mein Feedback turnt dich ab.
Du sagst, dass ich ein Wellness-Weekend dringend nötig hab.
Du sagst, ich käm' mit good Vibrations wieder in den Flow.
Du sagst, ich brauche Energy. Und ich denk: „Das sagst du so …"
Statt Nachrichten bekomme ich den Infotainment-Flash.
Ich sehne mich nach Bargeld, doch man gibt mir nicht mal Cash.
Ich fühl' mich beim Communicating unsicher wie nie –
da nützt mir auch kein Bodyguard. Ich brauch Security!

Ich will, dass beim Coffee-Shop „Kaffeehaus" oben draufsteht,
oder dass beim Auto-Crash die „Lufttasche" aufgeht,
und schön wär's, wenn wir Bodybuilder „Muskel-Mäster" nennen
und wenn nur noch „Nordisch Geher" durch die Landschaft rennen …

(Text und Melodie: Daniel Dickopf, Edition WISE GUYS, Köln)

> What is special about the song "Denglisch"?
> Describe.

englische Begriffe erkennen

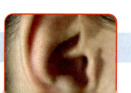

I can speak English

At the supermarket

Paul: Hey Emily, I must go shopping. Do you come with me?

Emily: Yes, of course. That is a good idea.

 1. Which other things do you know that sound English? Make a list.

 2. Collect pictures from magazines that show a "denglish" word. Make a collage.

3. Present your collage.

englische Begriffe erkennen

1 Welcome to English:

English around the world

This is a world map.
It shows where people speak English.

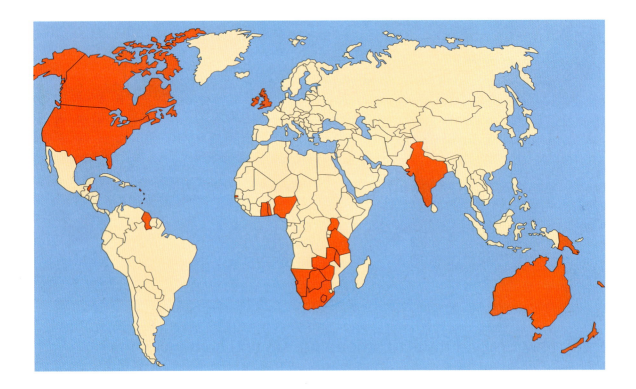

 Use an atlas.
Can you find the names of the countries in red?

sich über die Weltsprache Englisch austauschen

I can speak English

The pupils from my class

 Where do the pupils from your class come from?
Ask your neighbour and mark a map.

die Herkunft der Mitschüler erfragen

2   About me:

You and I

2 About me:

Rock around the clock

Track 02

    1 2   3   4

One two three o'clock four o'clock rock

    5 6   7   8

five six seven o'clock eight o'clock rock

    9 10 11   12

nine ten eleven o'clock twelve o'clock rock

we're gonna rock around the clock tonight

(Text und Melodie: Max C. Freedman/Jimmy de Knight; © Myers Music Inc., Edition Kassner & Co., Musikverlag Tuzlingen)

Listen and sing.

Zahlen von 1 bis 12 kennenlernen

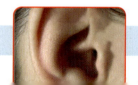

You and I

Hello

Introduce yourself:

My name is …

I am … years old.

I am from …

sich vorstellen

2 About me:

Meeting friends

Track 03

Emily: Hello. I am Emily.
          What is your name?

Paul: Hi, my name is Paul.
          I am twelve years old.
          How old are you?

Emily: I am eleven years old.
          Where are you from?

Paul: I am from Bristol.

Emily: I am from Bristol, too.

And you?
Can you answer the questions?

name: What is your name?
age: How old are you?
from: Where are you from?

16   sich bekannt machen

You and I

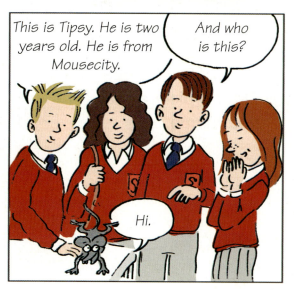

Introduce your friend.

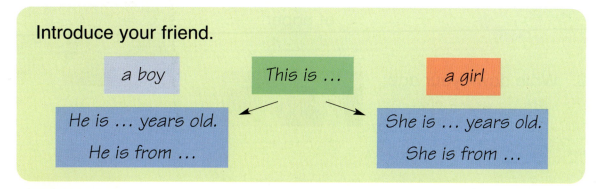

jemanden vorstellen

2   About me:

This is me

Collect things for your book:
- 6 sheets of A4-sized paper
- 2 sheets of card (A4-sized)
- a puncher
- glue
- string
- photos of yourself
- photos/postcards of your city

Now make your me-book!

1. Draw a picture with your name.

2. Glue the photos on a sheet of paper.

3. Write down your age:
   I am ... years old.

Auskunft erteilen

You and I

4. Glue the photo(s) of your city on a sheet of paper.
   Write: *This is ...*

5. Make the cover: Draw a picture with the title "me-book".

6. Glue it onto the card.

7. Punch holes into the cards and the paper.

8. Fix it with a string.

Finished!

Show your me-book to the class.

Auskunft erteilen

2 About me:

Strategy:
How to make word cards

Side 1:
Write down the
English word.
Draw a picture.

Side 2:
Write down the
German word.
Draw a picture.

Put the cards
into a box.

Learn the words.

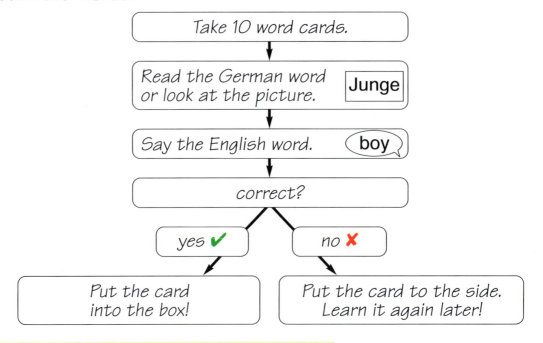

You can play games with the cards, too.
Ask your teacher!

You and I

This is what you have learned

1. Numbers

Count ⇑:   1 – 2 – 3 – …
Count ⇓:   12 – 11 – 10 – …

2. Who is this?

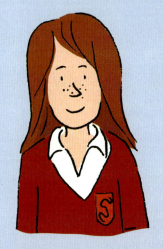  

This is …   This …   …
She is … years old. He …   …
She is from …   He …   …

3. Questions and answers

What is your name?
How old are you?
Where are you from?

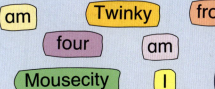

21

3 At school:

Our classroom

3 At school:

The colour of the classroom

Track 05

Emily's and Paul's class want to paint their classroom. They discuss the new colour of the classroom.

Paul: I like green. Green is fresh.
Emily: I like yellow. Yellow is friendly.
Robin: I like blue. Blue is nice.

Which colour do you like?

24   Vorlieben ausdrücken

Our classroom

Renovation week

Monday: clean classroom
Tuesday: carry out chairs and tables
Wednesday: buy paint
Thursday: paint wall
Friday: decorate classroom
Saturday: party
Sunday: day off

Which job do you want to do?
I want to paint the wall on Thursday.

Wochentage

3 At school:

A riddle

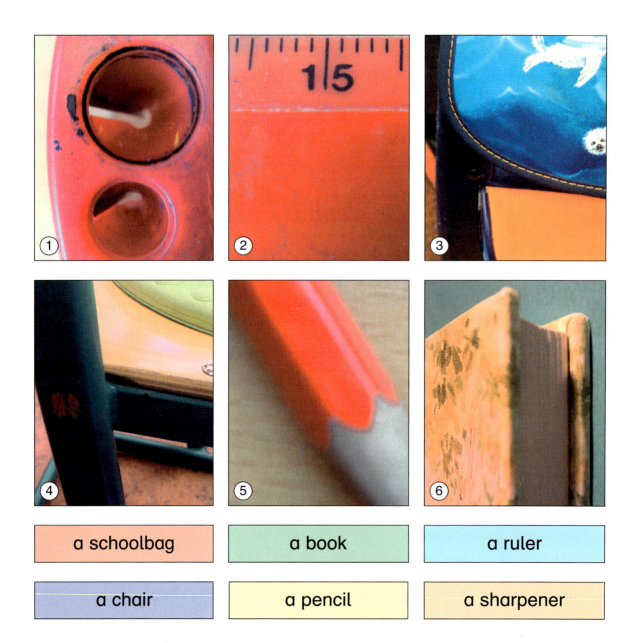

Be a detective. What is it?

Number 1 is a …

Schule

Our classroom

Schoolthings-chant

Track 06

Have you got a pencil? Yes, I have.

Have you got a ruler? Yes, I have.

Have you got a pencil-case? Yes, I have.

Have you got a schoolbag? Yes, I have.

Have you got a sharpener? Yes, I have.

Have you got a friend? Yes, I have.

Here she/he is.

Speak:
angrily,
loudly,
whisper,
like a witch,
like a monster …

Besitzverhältnisse ausdrücken

3 At school:

I see a girl …

Play this game in your class.

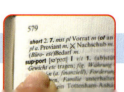

Farben

Our classroom

Everything is gone!

under

between

in

on

Where are Emily's things?
The rubber is under the desk.
The ruler is …

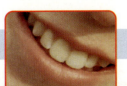

Auskunft erteilen

3 At school:

Strategy:
Well organised?

Be well organised and learn better.

My	glue	is	in	the chair.
	pencil		on	the table.
	rubber		under	the desk.
	book		between	the schoolbag.
	ruler		at	the pencil-case.
	sharpener			the folder.
	pen			home.

 What about you?
Write down three sentences.
Present your work.

30

Our classroom

This is what you have learned

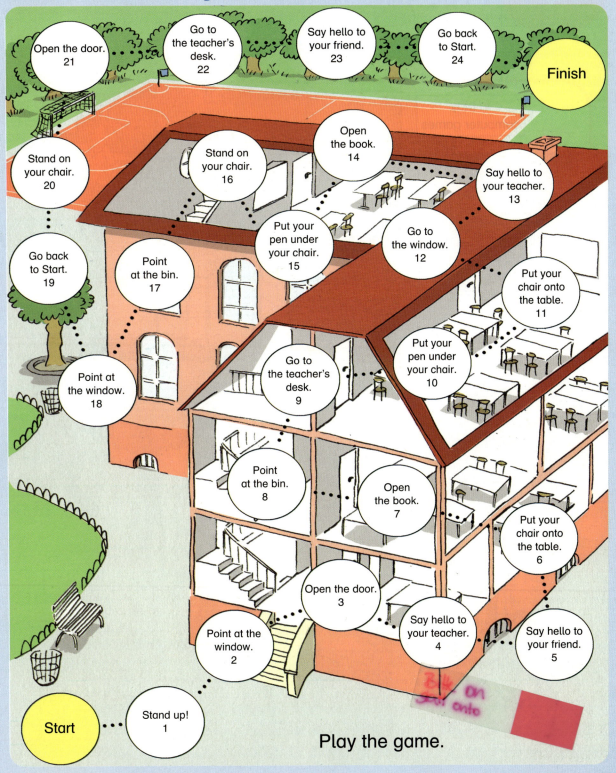

Play the game.

I like ...
He likes ....

to swim
to listen to music
to cycle
to watch TV
to play table tennis
to draw
to skateboard

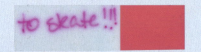

to skate!!!

Sports and hobbies

4 Free time:

What about you-rap

I like to read.
What about you?
I like to dance.
What about you?
I like to draw.
What about you?
I like to swim.
What about you?
I like to cycle.
What about you?
I like to sing.
And what do **you** do?

 Repeat the rap and answer.

Vorlieben ausdrücken

Sports and hobbies

What are their hobbies?

Betty

Tom and Marc

Betty likes to play soccer.

… like to watch TV.

… likes to ride a horse.

… like to play table tennis.

… like to play basketball.

… like to go inline skating.

Linda and John

Robin

Emily and Paul

Jim and Sarah

What are their hobbies?
Match! Read the sentence.

Aktivitäten beschreiben

35

4 Free time:

Interview about hobbies

Track 09

This is Mandy.

Mandy is eleven years old.

She writes for a pupils' magazine.

She interviews her classmates about their hobbies.

These are her notes.

	Kate	Rob
to play computer games	☹	☺
to listen to music	☺	☹
to play table tennis	☹	☺
to play basketball	☺	☹
to swim	☺	☹

Listen to the interview.

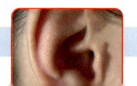

Vorlieben/Abneigungen ausdrücken

Sports and hobbies

Hi, I am Mandy.
I write for our school magazine.
May I ask you some questions about your hobbies, Kate?
Do you like to play computer games?

No, I do not. ☹

Do you like to listen to music?

Yes, I do. ☺

Do you like to play table tennis?

No, I do not. ☹
I hate table tennis. ☹

Do you like to play basketball?

Yes, I do. ☺
I love basketball. ☺

I like to swim. What about you?

I like to swim, too. ☺

Thank you very much, Kate.

1. Read again.
2. Act the interview.

Vorlieben/Abneigungen ausdrücken

4 Free time:

Strategy:
How to do an interview

1.
Write down short questions.

2.
Look for an interview partner.

3.
Introduce yourself.

4.
Ask friendly. ☺

5.
Ask clearly.

6.
Write down the answers.

7.
Say thank you.

Prepare your own interview.
Start like this:

I am …
May I ask you some questions?
Do you like …?

Sports and hobbies

A class interview

This is the result of our class interview about hobbies. Nine pupils like to play soccer. Four pupils like to dance …

Go on.
What about your class?
 Do a class interview.

Informationen über Hobbys einholen

4 Free time:

This is what you have learned

1. Put your counters at START.

2. The one who throws a six starts.

3. Roll the dice again.

4. Go.

5. Word: Play the hobby.

6. Look for the next matching picture and move there.

7. Now it is the next one's turn.

8. And so on …

9. Picture: Say the hobby.

10. Miss a turn, throw again.

11. Who is first at FINISH?

Sports and hobbies

5 My body:

Descriptions

5 My body:

At the mirror cabinet

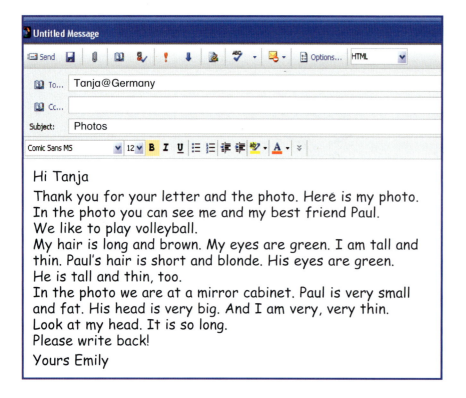

Hi Tanja
Thank you for your letter and the photo. Here is my photo.
In the photo you can see me and my best friend Paul.
We like to play volleyball.
My hair is long and brown. My eyes are green. I am tall and thin. Paul's hair is short and blonde. His eyes are green. He is tall and thin, too.
In the photo we are at a mirror cabinet. Paul is very small and fat. His head is very big. And I am very, very thin. Look at my head. It is so long.
Please write back!
Yours Emily

Emily writes an e-mail to a friend in Germany.

1. Read the text.
2. Describe Emily and Paul.

44   sich selbst und andere beschreiben

Descriptions

A new page in your me-book!

You need:
- 2 sheets of A4-sized paper
- glue
- a photo of yourself
- a photo of your best friend

1. Glue your photo onto a new page.
   Write: *This is me. My hair is …*

What do you look like?
My hair is …	black/red/brown/blonde
My eyes are …	blue/green/brown
I am …	small/tall/fat/thin

2. Glue the photo of your friend onto a new page.
   Write: *This is my best friend …*

And your best friend?
A boy?	His hair is …	His eyes …	He is …
A girl?	Her hair …	Her eyes …	She is …

1. Put the pages in your me-book!
2. Find a partner.
   Tell him or her about you and your best friend.

sich selbst und andere beschreiben

5 My body:

Who is who?

| Mandy | David | Kate | Robin |

Track 11

Listen to the CD.

Find the name of the girl in picture 1.
Find the name of the boy in picture 2.
Find the name of the girl in picture 3.
Find the name of the boy in picture 4.

46 Beschreibungen verstehen und zuordnen

Descriptions

Parts of the body

1. Listen to the song.
2. Can you touch the parts of your body along with the song?

Head and shoulders, knees and toes,
knees and toes,
knees and toes,
head and shoulders, knees and toes,
it's my body!

Eyes and ears and mouth and nose,
mouth and nose,
mouth and nose,
eyes and ears and mouth and nose,
it's my body!

Head and shoulders, knees and toes,
knees and toes,
knees and toes,
head and shoulders, knees and toes,
it's my body!

(Text und Melodie: überliefert aus England)

Track 12

Körperteile

5 My body:

Alien

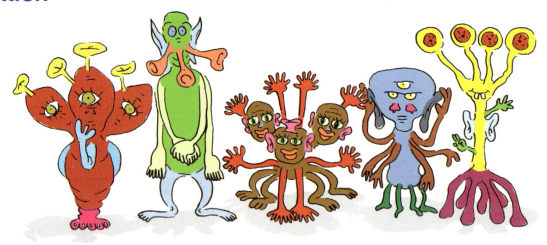

This is Mibi, the alien. She is from the planet Mars.
On Mars, all aliens have a lot of heads, eyes, ears, noses, mouths, arms, fingers and legs.

Mibi has got three heads.
She has got six eyes. Her eyes are green.
She has got two noses. Her noses are blue.
She has got seven ears. Her ears are purple.
She has got three mouths. Her mouths are orange.
Her body is brown.
She has got eight arms with seven fingers.
Her arms and fingers are red.
She has got four legs. Her legs are brown.

1. Can you find Mibi?
 2. The names of the other aliens are Mobi, Mubi, Mabi and Mebi. Choose one alien and tell your class about it.

Personen beschreiben

Descriptions

Alien gallery

1. Take a sheet of A4-sized paper.
2. Draw your alien:
    - Roll the dice: This is the number of eyes.
    - Roll the dice: This is the number of ears.
    - Roll the dice: This is the number of noses.
    - Roll the dice: This is the number of mouths.
    - Roll the dice: This is the number of arms.
    - Roll the dice: This is the number of legs.
    - Roll the dice: This is the number of fingers.

3. Do not forget to colour in your alien!
4. Give it a name.

Körperteile benennen

49

5 My body:

Strategy:
Tell your class

Sometimes you must tell your class the results of your work.
This is how you can do it.

1. What can you say?
   Write it down. ⟶

2. How can you say it?
   Learn it with a partner.

3. Stand in front of the class.
   Speak loudly and slowly.

Look at the class.

My alien
name: Gobo
heads: 2
hair: blue and pink
eyes: 3, red
noses: 2, green
arms: 4, yellow

*This is my alien.
His name is Gobo.
He has got two heads.
His hair is blue and pink.
He has got three eyes.
The eyes are red …*

 Now tell your class about your alien.
Can they find it in the alien gallery?

Descriptions

This is what you have learned

White: What can you see?
Correct?   Roll again.
Wrong?   Go back two steps.

Red: Miss a turn.

Blue: Check the sentence.
Sentence true?   Roll again.
Sentence false? Go back two steps.

Purple: Go forwards two steps.

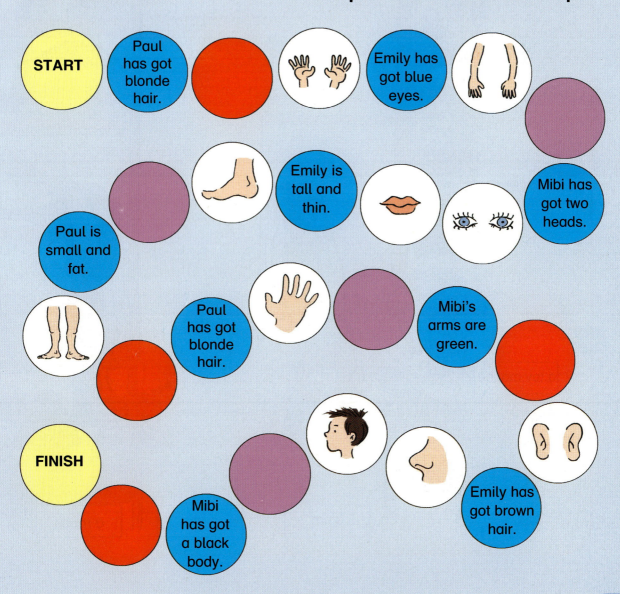

6 Pets and animals:

Our pets

6 Pets and animals:

My pet

The class talks about its pets.

> This is my cat Teddy.
> He is six months old.
> He is grey.
> He likes to play with a toy mouse.
> He drinks water and eats cat food.
> He likes milk, too.
> He sleeps in my bed.

Track 14

1. Listen to the text.
2. Read the text again.
3. What can you say about Teddy?

Tiere beschreiben

Our pets

More pets

Tell your class about these pets.

hamster
name: Sammy
age: 10 months
colour: brown and white
likes to: run in his hamster wheel
eats: hamster food
drinks: water
sleeps: in a cage

rabbit
name: Molly
age: 2 years
colour: brown and black
likes to: run in the grass
eats: carrots, grass
drinks: water
sleeps: in a cage

Tiere beschreiben

55

6 Pets and animals:

Pet interview

Emily asks her class.
Paul makes notes.

  1. Now interview your class.
  2. Write down the results.

Fragen einüben

Our pets

What Paul and Emily found out

Paul tells his class the results of the interview.

Track 15

> Eight pupils have got pets.
> Four pupils have not got pets.
> Peggy has got a rabbit.
> Harry has got two rabbits.
> Sally has got a budgie.
> Ron has got three budgies.
> Sarah and Emily have got dogs.
> Michael has not got a pet,
> but he likes dogs.
> Emma has not got a pet,
> but she likes dogs, too.
> Norman and Wilma have not
> got pets, but they like
> horses and birds.

1. Listen to Paul.
2. Look at **your** interview notes.
3. What can you say about **your** class?

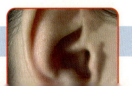

Auskunft erteilen

57

6 Pets and animals

Strategy:
Our animal exhibition

Posters are a great way to inform about an animal. Here is how you can make one.

Take a sheet of A3-sized paper, glue, pens and a photo of your pet.

Write down the title.

Glue the photo onto the paper.

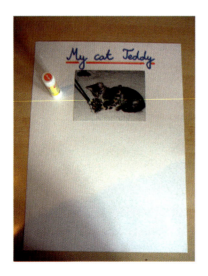

Write the categories on the paper.

Our pets

Fill in the information.

Draw pictures next to new words.

Pin the poster on the wall.
You can tell your class about your pet now!

6 Pets and animals:

This is what you have learned

Our pets

Can you help the boy and build a bridge for all the animals? Take four stones and make a sentence.

7 Around the house:

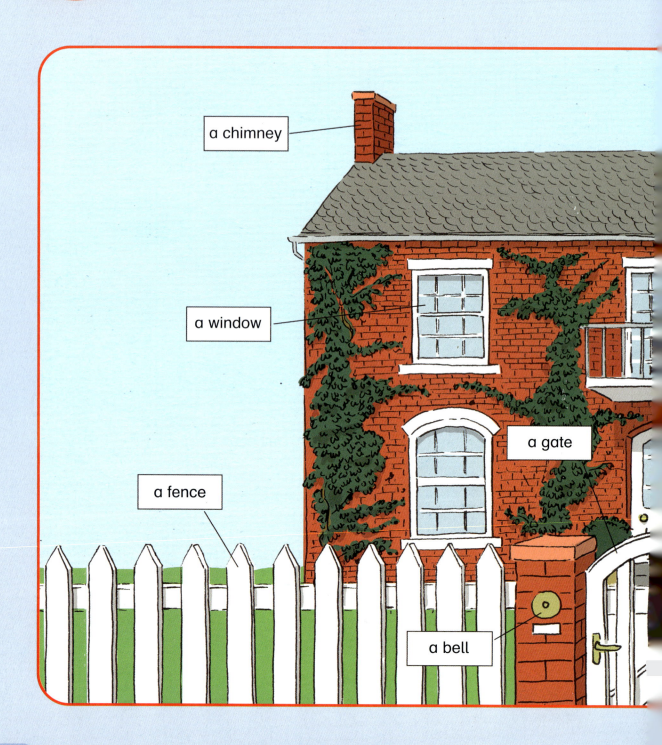

At home

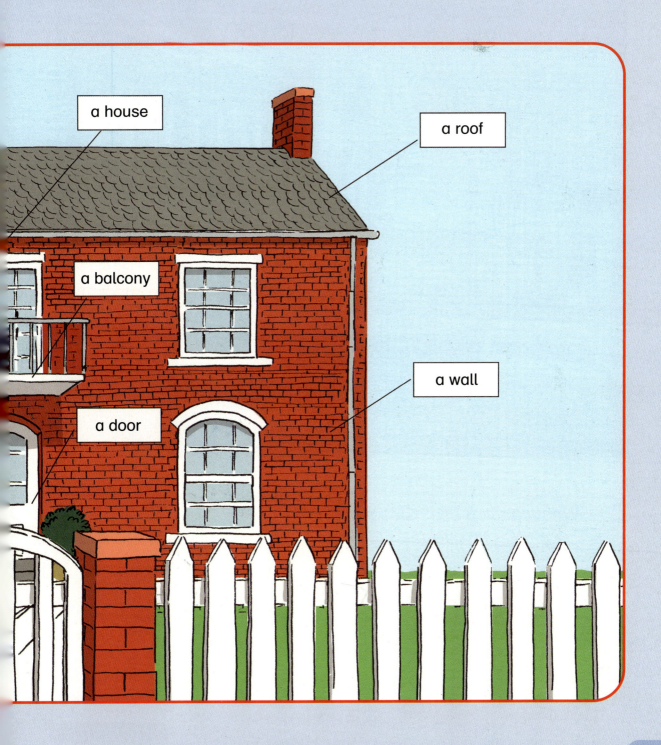

7 Around the house:

How people live

1. What can you see? Describe!

   I can see a/an ...

2. Would you like to live here?
   Say why or why not.

   I would like to live here, because ...
   I would not like to live here, because ...

64 Gegenstände beschreiben

At home

Paul's new home

Hello reader! This is where I will live. It is nice, so my parents want to move.

1. Draw your "dream house".
   Use the words to name the parts:
   a house – a wall – a door – a window – a roof –
   a chimney – a balcony – a fence – a gate – a bell

 2. Present your house to the class.

Gegenstände beschreiben

7 Around the house:

Moving house

1. Name the furniture.
   Use the following words:
   a chair – a table – a cupboard – a couch – a wardrobe – a television – a carpet – a bed

Möbel

At home

The new house

This is a plan of the house where Paul and his family will live in.

Read the text.

Here is what you have to do when you move house:
You must take down the furniture and put it up again.
You must pack all your books, toys and clothes into many boxes and unpack them later.
Finally, enjoy your new home.

Track 17

Haus

7 Around the house:

A designing project

 1. Copy the plan of the house onto a big sheet of paper.

2. Arrange the pictures from the magazines in any room.

 3. Present your results to the class.

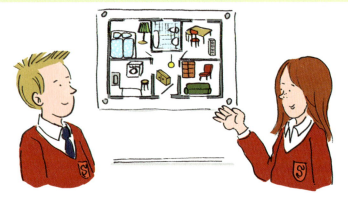

Vorlieben ausdrücken

7 At home

Strategy:
Writing an e-mail

Track 18

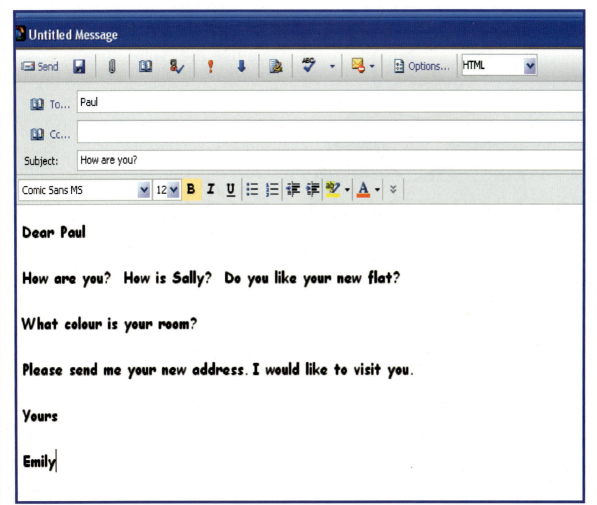

1. Now answer Emily's e-mail. You can start like this:

   Dear Emily
   Thank you very much for your letter.
   I am fine. …

7 Around the house:

Paul will live somewhere new

To say things in future tense, we use the "will-future".

Track 19

When you want to move,
you will have to decide where you want to live.
Will you live in a house?
Will you live in a flat?
Will you have your own room?
There will be a lot to do.
 Good friends will always help you.

 Have you ever moved into a new home?
Discuss in class.

sich über Zukünftiges austauschen

At home

This is what you have learned

- Form two teams.

- Write rooms (kitchen, bathroom, …) onto cards.

- Each team takes a card.

- Look at the card and read it out.

- The other team names as much furniture which belongs to this room as possible.

- Which team names more? It wins!

Good luck …

8 Around town:

Going places

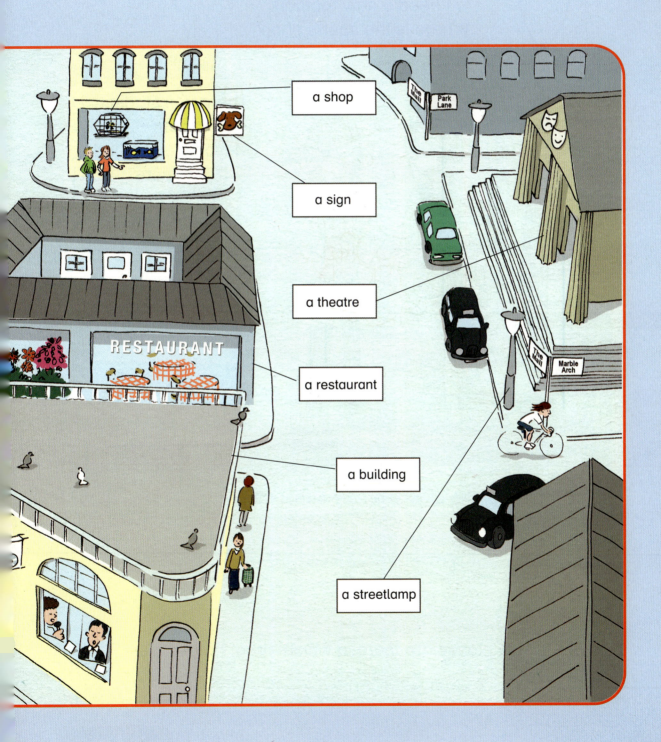

8   Around town:

What is where?

1. Look for the places on the street map.
   Which place is in which street?
   Try to make short dialogues.

   - Where is the ...?
   - The ... is in ... Street.

2. Which places are there in which street? Make a list.

   — In Book Street, there are a bookshop and a factory.

sich nach dem Standort erkundigen

Going places

Fragestruktur mit „Where …?"/Wortschatzerweiterung

8   Around town:

Out and about in the city

Track 20

Emily and Paul are on their way into town.

Paul: What shall we do now? Have you got an idea?
Emily: How about an ice-cream?

On their way, they meet a man who is lost.

Man: Excuse me, where is the supermarket?
Paul: The supermarket is in Oxford Street.
Man: Is that far from here?
Emily: No, it is not. It is just around the corner.
Man: Thank you very much. Good bye.
Paul & Emily: You are welcome. Good bye.

> 1. Read the dialogue.
> 2. Where is the supermarket?

Auskunft erteilen

8 Going places

Strategy:
Reading a map

1. Walk from the car park in Prince Street to a restaurant in Corn Street. Describe your way.
2. What is a legend and what is special about it? Collect your ideas.

Here is a street map of Bristol.

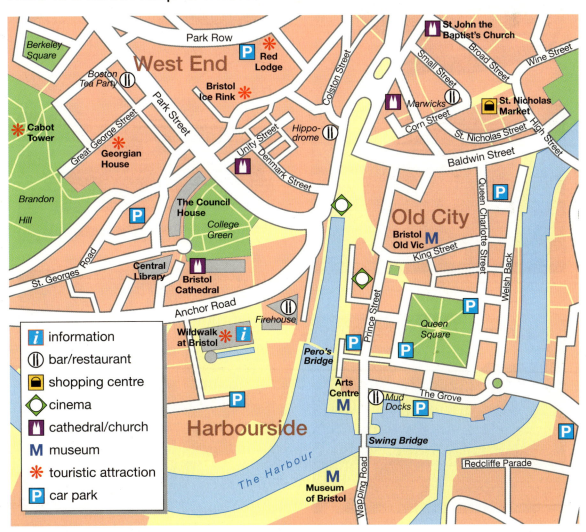

8 Around town:

Means of transportation

In a city, there are many ways to go from A to B.
Sometimes you do not even need a car.

mit dem Wörterbuch arbeiten

Going places

1. Look up the means of transportation in a dictionary.
2. Draw pictures to explain the means of transportation. Follow the example. Use an A3-sized paper.
3. What means of transportation are in your town?

mit dem Wörterbuch arbeiten

8 Around town:

Looking for the music shop

Track 21

Paul and Emily are looking for the music shop.
Paul wants to buy a new CD.
Emily wants to have an ice-cream.
They go into the music shop to buy the CD.

Emily: Well, you have your CD. Now I would like an ice-cream.
Shall we take the bus?

Paul: The tube will be much quicker.
You are always in traffic jams when you use the bus.

Emily: You are right. Let us take the tube.

The friends go and have a nice ice-cream.

1. Read the text carefully.
2. What is Paul's argument to take the tube?

einen Text inhaltlich erfassen können

Going places

This is what you have learned

BINGO

– Each pupil has one sheet of paper with words of this chapter on it.

– There are different versions of the sheet of paper.

– The teacher reads the words one by one.

– The pupils must cross out the words that they have.

– The first pupil who crosses out all the words wins the game.

Good luck …

9 Around the world:

82

Education in Great Britain

9 Around the world:

School in Great Britain

What is special about pupils in Great Britain? Describe!

Pupils in Great Britain wear …

Informationen austauschen

Education in Great Britain

Designing a new school uniform

1. You are the designer.
   Dress Emily and Paul.
   Design a new uniform.
2. Which colours do you use?
 3. Present your design to the class.

Arbeitsergebnisse vorstellen

9 Around the world:

Paul's timetable

Time	Monday	Tuesday	Wednesday	Thursday	Friday
08:25	compulsory daily registration I				
08:50 - 09:50	Technology	Business	English	Maths	English
09:50 - 10:50	Technology	IT	IT	Science	Media
10:50 - 11:10	break				
11:10 - 12:10	Drama	Science	Media	Science	Maths
12:10 - 13:10	Maths	Maths	Technology	Media	Drama
13:10 - 14:05	lunch				
14:05	compulsory daily registration II				
14:15 - 15:15	English	English	Drama	Business	Business

1. You can see Paul's timetable. Compare it to your timetable.
2. Which subjects do you know? Which subjects do you not know?
3. Which subjects do you like, which do you not like?

88   sich über Vorlieben/Abneigungen austauschen

9   Education in Great Britain

Strategy:
Pros and cons

Tables are very practical.
They **give** you a **structure**.

School in Great Britain

- to leave school late
- to look the same every day
- to wear a uniform
- to wear a tie every day
- to have lunch at school
- to choose clothes for school
- to have school in the afternoon
- to start school late

The pros:	The cons:
– to start school late – to have lunch at school – …	– to leave school late – …

1. Divide the list into pro and contra the British school system.
2. Copy the table and complete.

9 Around the world:

School uniforms

> 1. What do you think? Is the text pro or contra school uniforms?
> Read carefully.

Track 22

Uniforms can be very useful.
Most of the pupils in Great Britain
like their uniforms.
They like to belong to a group.

Each school has its own uniform.
They have different colours.

Pupils wear a school uniform,
because every person wearing it is equal.

Many other countries have school uniforms.
They are for example India, Australia, Singapore, Hong Kong,
New Zealand, Cyprus and South Africa.
They are all former British colonies.

> 2. Can you find the countries from the text on a map of the world?

einen Sachtext verstehen

Education in Great Britain

This is what you have learned

A discussion:

- Form two teams.

- Write arguments pro and contra school uniforms onto cards.

- One team is pro, one is contra.

> Every person is equal! Uniforms show that.

- Look at the card and read it out.

> There is no room for individual taste.

- Try to lead a discussion in class about the necessity of school uniforms.

> …

- You can also change the subject:
  What about the British school system in general?
  Think of the table you made.

10 Around the year:

a celebration

a pumpkin

a ghost

an Easter bunny

92

Halloween, Christmas, Easter

10 Around the year:

Witch, witch come to my party!

Track 23

"Witch, Witch, please, come to my party."

"Thank you, I will, if you invite Cat."

"Dragon, Dragon, please, come to my party."

"Thank you, I will, if you invite Pirate."

Geschichten verstehen

Halloween

Listen and point to the pictures.

Geschichten verstehen

95

10 Around the year:

Halloween night

Act the rhyme.

einen Reim auswendig lernen

Halloween

About Halloween

Halloween is on the 31st of October.

A long time ago, this date marked

the beginning of the **New Year**.

People had masks and made fire

to frighten away **witches** and **ghosts**.

Today, on the evening of October the 31st,

children go from **house** to house.

Many children dress up as **ghosts**,

dragons, vampires, witches, skeletons, etc.

They ask for **sweets, nuts,** money, etc.

If they do not get anything, they play **tricks**.

Some **families** decorate their houses with **pumpkins**.

People have special parties where they play

Halloween games.

Track 25

---

1. Listen and read the text.
2. Look up words which you do not know in the dictionary.

landeskundliche Informationen lesen

10 Around the year:

Celebrating Christmas

1. How do you decorate your living-room for Christmas?
   Use a shoe box and decorate it.
   You can make a Christmas tree,
   you can make presents, …

seine Meinung äußern

Christmas

Christmas in Great Britain

In Great Britain, children have to wait for their presents until the 25th of December. Father Christmas has to put them into stockings.

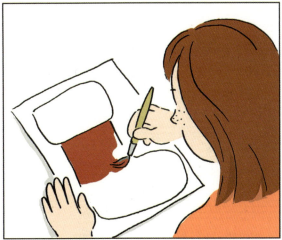

Draw a stocking.

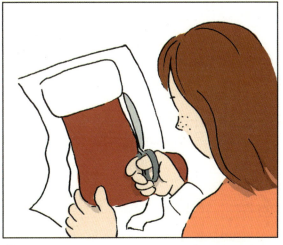

Cut it out.

Cut out pictures of presents.

Glue them at the back of the stocking. Finished!

Make your own stocking.
The pictures will help you.

Arbeitsanweisungen befolgen

10 Around the year:

Jingle Bells

Track 26

(Text und Melodie: James Lord Pierpont)

Listen to the CD.
Then sing the song.

ein Lied hören und singen

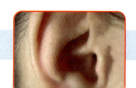

Christmas

Christmas in other countries

There are different ways to celebrate Christmas around the world.

- We celebrate Christmas.
- I do not like Christmas.
- I get my presents on the 24th of December.
- We visit friends and relatives.
- We have something special to eat.
- Friends and relatives visit us.
- It is just a normal day.
- I get my presents on the 25th of December.
- I like Christmas.
- We do not celebrate Christmas. We celebrate …

1. How do you celebrate Christmas in your family? The balloons will help you.
2. Some families do not celebrate Christmas. What do **you** celebrate? What is important for **you**?

Traditionen miteinander vergleichen

101

10   Around the year:

Celebrating Christmas

1. What can you see in the picture? Describe.
   I can see ...
2. Choose five things. Describe where they are.
   *The mistletoe is **on** the mantelpiece.*

Ortsangaben machen

Easter

The cress eggs

You need:
- cress seed
- eggs (blown out)
- tissues
- 1 wooden stick
- 2 glasses

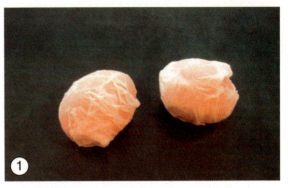

Fold damp tissues around the eggs.

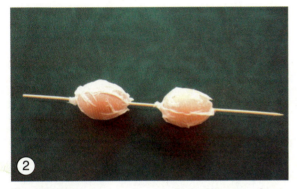

Push the wooden stick through the eggs.

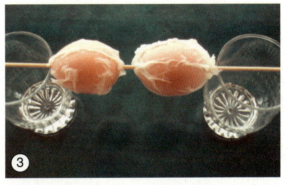

Put the wooden stick onto two glasses.

Spread the cress seed over the eggs. Water it every day.

Ready!

Follow the instructions to make the cress eggs.

Handlungsanweisungen verstehen und umsetzen

103

11 Grammar:

To play with language

11 Grammar:

To play with language – mit Sprache spielen

Jedes Spiel folgt bestimmten Spielregeln.
Diese Spielregeln musst du kennen und beachten,
damit das Spiel funktioniert.
Ähnlich ist es mit den Sprachen.
Die englische Sprache folgt bestimmten Regeln der Grammatik.
Wenn du diese Regeln kennst, fällt es dir leichter,
eine Sprache zu lernen.
Auf den folgenden Seiten findest du zunächst einige
Sprachforscher-Aufgaben (S.108 – 113), um mit Sprache zu spielen
und die Spielregeln der englischen Sprache kennenzulernen.
Im Anschluss folgt eine Zusammenfassung der Spielregeln
(S.114 – 125): die englische Grammatik.

Grammatik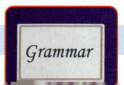

To play with language

Folgende Tabelle hilft dir, schwierige Wörter besser zu verstehen.

Deutsch	Fachbegriff	Englisch
Hauptwort (Namenwort)	Nomen (Substantiv)	noun
Einzahl	Singular	singular
Mehrzahl	Plural	plural
Tätigkeitswort, (Tuwort, Zeitwort)	Verb	verb
Grundform	Infinitiv	infinitive
Eigenschaftswort (Wiewort)	Adjektiv	adjective
Verhältniswort	Präposition	preposition
persönliches Fürwort	Personalpronomen	personal pronoun
besitzanzeigendes Fürwort	Possessivpronomen	possessive pronoun
Gegenwart	Präsens	present tense
einfache Form der Gegenwart	einfaches Präsens	simple present
Vergangenheit	Präteritum	past tense
einfache Form der Vergangenheit	einfaches Präteritum	simple past
Zukunft	Futur	future tense
Zukunft mit "will"	Futur	will-future
Fragen mit Fragewörtern (Bestimmungsfragen)		questions with question words
Entscheidungsfragen		yes/no questions

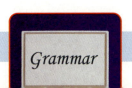

Grammatik

11 Grammar:

Sprachforscher-Aufgaben

1. *I, you, he, she, it –*
   das sind **persönliche Fürwörter** in der Einzahl.
   Wann benutzt man sie?
   Kannst du folgende Tabelle füllen?
   Übertrage die Tabelle in dein Heft.
   Ergänze sie mithilfe der Texte im zweiten Kapitel (About me) auf den Seiten 15 bis 17.

Was sagst du …	Deutsch	Englisch
… wenn du über dich selbst sprichst?		
… wenn du mit jemandem sprichst?		
… wenn du über einen Jungen sprichst?		
… wenn du über ein Mädchen sprichst?		
… wenn du über eine Sache sprichst?		

2. In der Einzahl hat das Tätigkeitswort **to be** *(sein)* drei Formen.
   Finde die Formen mithilfe der Texte im zweiten Kapitel (About me) auf den Seiten 16 und 17.
   Übertrage die Tabelle in dein Heft und ergänze sie.

Deutsch	Englisch
ich bin	
du bist	
er ist	
sie ist	
es ist	

Grammatik

To play with language

3. Im dritten Kapitel (At school) geht es um **Verhältniswörter** wie z.B. *in, on, at, between, under*.
   Suche sie im folgenden Text.
   Schreibe die Sätze in dein Heft und unterstreiche die Verhältniswörter.
   Was fällt dir auf? Hilfe findest du im Grammatikteil (S. 116).

   The rubber is in the pencil-case.
   The folder is on the table.
   The pen is under the book.
   The glue is at home.
   The ruler is between the pages.

4. Lege mit deinem Nachbarn ein Sammelplakat an.
   Welche **Verhältniswörter** kennt ihr? Fangt so an:

Verhältniswort	Beispiel
in	in the classroom
…	…

5. Lies dir die Sätze im vierten Kapitel (Free time) auf Seite 35 durch.
   Das Wort *like* verändert sich in der **einfachen Form der Gegenwart**.
   Finde heraus, **wann** und **wie** es sich verändert.
   Schreibe deine Beobachtung in dein Heft.
   Vergleiche sie mit deinem Nachbarn.

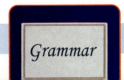

Grammatik

11 Grammar:

6. Du hast im zweiten Kapitel die persönlichen Fürwörter kennengelernt. Im fünften Kapitel (My body) geht es um die **besitzanzeigenden Fürwörter** *my, your, his, her, its, our, your, their*. Zu welchen persönlichen Fürwörtern gehören diese besitzanzeigenden Fürwörter? Lege in deinem Heft eine Tabelle an.

persönliches Fürwort	besitzanzeigendes Fürwort
I	my
...	...

7. Was beschreibt man mit den **besitzanzeigenden Fürwörtern**? Finde die Antwort mithilfe der Texte im fünften Kapitel (My body) auf den Seiten 44 und 48.

8. Wenn du über mehrere Sachen sprichst, benutzt du die **Mehrzahl**.
   Suche aus dem Bild auf Seite 42 und 43 zehn Körperteile heraus.
   Schreibe sie in deinem Heft untereinander auf.
   Suche dann mithilfe der folgenden Seiten des fünften Kapitels die passenden Mehrzahlformen heraus und schreibe sie hinter das Wort.
   Unterstreiche den letzten Buchstaben. Was fällt dir auf?
   Sprich mit deinem Nachbarn über deine Beobachtung.
   Versucht gemeinsam, einen Merksatz zu formulieren und schreibt ihn in euer Heft.

Grammatik

To play with language

9. Schau dir folgende Sätze an.
   Sie beschreiben, was jemand hat oder besitzt.

   > I have got a budgie.
   > Peter has got green eyes.
   > Emily has got a dog.
   > You have got black hair.

   Finde auf Seite 48 weitere Beispiele, in denen beschrieben wird, was jemand hat oder besitzt. Schreibe fünf Beispiele in dein Heft.
   Was fällt dir auf?

10. Wie sagt man, dass jemand etwas nicht hat oder nicht besitzt? Im sechsten Kapitel (Pets and animals) auf Seite 56 findest du ein Beispiel dafür. Schreibe den Beispielsatz in dein Heft und vergleiche ihn mit den Beispielen aus der vorherigen Aufgabe. Was fällt dir nun auf?

11. Wie kannst du etwas **Zukünftiges** ausdrücken?
    Schau dir die Seite 70 im siebten Kapitel (Around the house) an.
    Welches Wort wird in jedem Satz benutzt?
    Vergleiche dein Ergebnis mit dem Hinweis und den Beispielen im Grammatikteil auf Seite 122.
    Ist deine Vermutung richtig?

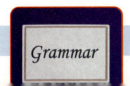

Grammatik

11 Grammar:

12. Im achten Kapitel (Around town) geht es um **Fragewörter**.
    Schreibe die folgenden Sätze in dein Heft.
    Unterstreiche in jedem Satz das Fragewort.
    Was fällt dir auf?

    What is your name?

    Where do you live?

    How old are you?

    When is your birthday?

    Which is your favourite hobby?

    Why is this your favourite hobby?

13. Lege in deinem Heft eine Tabelle mit den **Fragewörtern** an und versuche, das deutsche Wort zu finden.

Englisch	Deutsch
what	
where	
how	
when	
which	
why	

To play with language

14. Im neunten Kapitel (Around the world) wird auf Seite 86 von Claras Besuch im letzten Jahr erzählt.
    Wie kann man etwas **Vergangenes** ausdrücken?
    Was fällt dir an folgenden Sätzen über die Vergangenheit auf?

    Clara stayed with Paul last year.
    She visited Paul's school.
    Every day, they played football.
    She liked it very much.

    Hilfe findest du im Grammatikteil auf Seite 124.

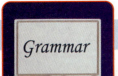

Grammatik

11 Grammar:

Zusammenfassung der Sprachregeln

Kapitel 2: Persönliche Fürwörter

Wenn du über dich, über Personen oder mit jemandem sprichst, benutzt du die **persönlichen Fürwörter.**

	Du sprichst …	Dann sagst du …
I	… über dich selbst?	… ich (*I*).
you	… jemanden an?	… du/Sie (*you*).
he	… über eine männliche Person?	… er (*he*).
she	… über eine weibliche Person?	… sie (*she*).
it	… über einen Gegenstand oder ein Tier, das du nicht beim Namen nennst?	… er/sie/es (*it*).
we	… über eine Gruppe von Leuten, zu der du selbst gehörst?	… wir (*we*).
you	… mehrere Leute an?	… ihr/Sie (*you*).
they	… über mehrere Leute?	… sie (*they*).

I am from London. (*Ich* komme aus London.)
You are from Munich. (*Du* kommst aus München.)
Where are **you** from? (Woher kommst *du*?)
She is ten years old. (*Sie* ist zehn Jahre alt.)

Grammatik

Summary

Die Formen von *to be*

Das Tätigkeitswort ***to be*** (sein) hat die drei Formen ***am, are, is***.
Achte darauf, über wen du sprichst.
Diese Formen musst du wie Vokabeln lernen.

Englisch		Deutsch	
I	*am*	Ich	bin
You	*are*	Du/Sie	bist/sind
He/Paul	*is*	Er	ist
She/Emily	*is*	Sie	ist
It	*is*	Er/Sie/Es	ist
We	*are*	Wir	sind
You	*are*	Ihr/Sie	seid/sind
They	*are*	Sie	sind

Paul *is* a boy. (Paul *ist* ein Junge.)
Emily *is* a girl. (Emily *ist* ein Mädchen.)
We *are* friends. (Wir *sind* Freunde.)

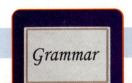

Grammatik

11 Grammar:

Kapitel 3: Verhältniswörter

Um zu sagen, wo sich etwas befindet, benutzt man **Verhältniswörter** wie z. B. *in, on, at, between, under*.
Sie stellen Verhältnisse zwischen Personen oder Gegenständen her und stehen vor einem Hauptwort.
Verhältniswörter haben häufig unterschiedliche Übersetzungen, je nach Situation.

Englisch	Deutsch
on Monday	*am* Montag
at the weekend	*am* Wochenende
in the morning	*am* Morgen

Da hilft nur
→ in einem Wörterbuch nachschlagen,
→ viel auf Englisch lesen und
→ wichtige Redewendungen mit Verhältniswörtern auswendig lernen.

Kapitel 4: Die einfache Form der Gegenwart

Um zu sagen, dass du etwas regelmäßig tust, z. B. ein Hobby, benutzt du die **einfache Form der Gegenwart**.
Die einfache Form der Gegenwart hat die gleiche Form wie die Grundform ohne *to*:

I *play* football. (Ich *spiele* Fußball.)

116 Grammatik

Summary

Bei *he/she/it* (3. Person Einzahl) wird an die Grundform noch ein -s angehängt:
He play**s** football. (Er spielt Fußball.)

Englisch			Deutsch		
I	*like*	music.	Ich	*mag*	Musik.
You	*like*	music.	Du Sie	*magst* *mögen*	Musik. Musik.
He	*likes*	music.	Er	*mag*	Musik.
She	*likes*	music.	Sie	*mag*	Musik.
It	*likes*	music.	Er/Sie/Es	*mag*	Musik.
We	*like*	music.	Wir	*mögen*	Musik.
You	*like*	music.	Ihr Sie	*mögt* *mögen*	Musik. Musik.
They	*like*	music.	Sie	*mögen*	Musik.

Die Verneinung der einfachen Gegenwart
Wenn du etwas in der Gegenwart verneinen möchtest, benutzt du **do not**. Bei *he/she/it* benutzt du **does not**:

We **do not** play basketball. (Wir spielen *kein* Basketball.)
She **does not** like music. (Sie mag *keine* Musik.)

Entscheidungsfragen
Wenn du von jemandem wissen möchtest, ob er etwas mag oder nicht mag, fragst du:

Do you like music? (*Magst du* Musik?)
Yes, I do./No, I do not.

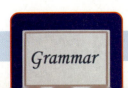

Grammatik

Kapitel 5: Besitzanzeigende Fürwörter

Wenn du über etwas sprichst, das dir oder zu dir gehört, benutzt du die **besitzanzeigenden Fürwörter**.

Englisch		Deutsch	
My	eyes are brown.	*Meine*	Augen sind braun.
Your	eyes are blue.	*Deine/Ihre*	Augen sind blau.
His	eyes are black.	*Seine*	Augen sind schwarz.
Her	eyes are green.	*Ihre*	Augen sind grün.
Its	eyes are yellow.	*Seine/Ihre*	Augen sind gelb.
Our	eyes are blue.	*Unsere*	Augen sind blau.
Your	eyes are brown.	*Eure/Ihre*	Augen sind braun.
Their	eyes are green.	*Ihre*	Augen sind grün.

Mit diesen besitzanzeigenden Fürwörtern kannst du sagen, (zu) wem etwas gehört oder zu wem jemand gehört:

This is *my* friend. (Dies ist *meine* Freundin.)

Her name is Kate. (*Ihr* Name ist Kate.)

Who is *your* friend? (Wer ist *dein* Freund?)

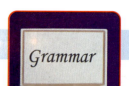

Summary

Die Mehrzahl der Hauptwörter

Wenn du über mehrere Gegenstände, Personen oder Tiere sprichst, benutzt du die **Mehrzahl**.
Du bildest die Mehrzahl, indem du an die Einzahl des Hauptwortes ein -s anhängst.

Englisch Einzahl	Englisch Mehrzahl	Deutsch Mehrzahl
one head –	three heads	drei Köpfe
one finger –	five fingers	fünf Finger
one leg –	two legs	zwei Beine
one shoulder –	two shoulders	zwei Schultern

Normalerweise hört man das *-e* am Ende eines Wortes nicht.
Aber in der Mehrzahl wird es mitgesprochen.

one nose   –   two   noses   (zwei Nasen)

Es gibt einige Ausnahmen bei der Mehrzahlbildung.
Diese musst du wie Vokabeln lernen.
Du findest diese Formen in der Vokabelliste.

one f*oo*t – two f*ee*t (zwei Füße)

one child – three child*ren* (drei Kinder)

Grammatik

11 Grammar:

Kapitel 6: Die Formen von *to have got/has got*

Wenn du sagen möchtest, dass du oder jemand anderes etwas hat oder besitzt, benutzt du das Tätigkeitswort **to have got** (etwas haben, besitzen).

In den meisten Fällen benutzt man die Form **have got**.

Nur wenn man über **eine** andere Person, **ein** Tier, **einen** Gegenstand oder **eine** Pflanze spricht, benutzt man die Form **has got**.

Englisch			Deutsch
I	*have got*	a budgie.	Ich *habe* einen Wellensittich.
You	*have got*	a budgie.	Du *hast* einen Wellensittich.
He/Paul	*has got*	a budgie.	Er *hat* einen Wellensittich.
She/Emily	*has got*	a budgie.	Sie *hat* einen Wellensittich.
It/The monster	*has got*	a budgie.	Es *hat* einen Wellensittich.
We	*have got*	a budgie.	Wir *haben* einen Wellensittich.
You	*have got*	a budgie.	Ihr *habt* einen Wellensittich.
They	*have got*	a budgie.	Sie *haben* einen Wellensittich.

You **have got** a mouse. (Du *hast* eine Maus.)

We **have got** hamsters. (Wir *haben* Hamster.)

Peter and Mary **have got** rabbits. (Peter und Mary *haben* Kaninchen.)

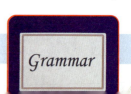

Summary

Wenn du sagen möchtest, dass du oder jemand anderes etwas nicht hat, musst du das Wort **not** einfügen.
Not steht immer zwischen *have/has* und dem Wort *got*.

Englisch			Deutsch
I	have *not* got	a budgie.	Ich habe *keinen* Wellensittich.
You	have *not* got	a budgie.	Du hast/Sie haben *keinen* Wellensittich.
He/Paul	has *not* got	a budgie.	Er hat *keinen* Wellensittich.
She/Emily	has *not* got	a budgie.	Sie hat *keinen* Wellensittich.
It/The monster	has *not* got	a budgie.	Es hat *keinen* Wellensittich.
We	have *not* got	a budgie.	Wir haben *keinen* Wellensittich.
You	have *not* got	a budgie.	Ihr habt/Sie haben *keinen* Wellensittich.
They	have *not* got	a budgie.	Sie haben *keinen* Wellensittich.

We **have not got** rabbits. (Wir *haben* keine Kaninchen.)

Emily **has not got** a cat. (Emily *hat* keine Katze.)

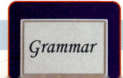

Grammatik

121

11 Grammar:

Kapitel 7: Die Zukunft mit *will*

Mit dem **will-future** (Zukunft) kannst du etwas Zukünftiges ausdrücken.
In folgenden Schritten gehst du vor:
1. Finde das Tätigkeitswort:
   He *moves* into a new flat. (Er *zieht* in eine neue Wohnung *ein*.)
2. Bilde die Grundform:
   He moves ⇒ *to move* (Er zieht ein ⇒ *einziehen*)
3. Setze die Grundform ohne *to* ein und füge *will* hinzu:
   He *will move* into a new flat.
   (Er *wird* in eine neue Wohnung *einziehen*.)

Englisch		Deutsch
I	*will move* into a new flat.	Ich *werde* in eine neue Wohnung *einziehen*.
We	*will have* a new address.	Wir *werden* eine neue Adresse *haben*.
Paul	*will meet* new people.	Paul *wird* neue Leute *kennenlernen*.
He	*will have* new neighbours.	Er *wird* neue Nachbarn *haben*.
Emily	*will visit* Paul in the new flat.	Emily *wird* Paul in der neuen Wohnung *besuchen*.

Beispiel für eine Frage im will-future:
Will he *move* into a new flat?   *Wird* er in eine neue Wohnung *einziehen*?

Kapitel 8: Fragen mit Fragewörtern

Mit **Fragewörtern** kannst du erfragen, was passiert, wo, warum, wann und wie es passiert. So gehst du vor:

1. Satz in der Gegenwart:
   I arrive at ten o'clock. (Ich komme um zehn Uhr an.)

2. Unterstreiche die Information, die du wissen möchtest.
   I arrive *at ten o'clock.* (Ich komme *um zehn Uhr* an.)

3. Wähle das richtige Fragewort:

Englisch	Deutsch
what?	was?
where?	wo?
why?	warum?
when?	*wann?*
how?	wie?
who?	wer? / wen?
which?	welches?

4. Stelle die Frage:
   When do you arrive? (*Wann* kommst du an?)

5. Beachte die Reihenfolge der Wörter. Die Fragewörter stehen immer am Anfang:
   I arrive at ten o'clock. ⇒ When do you arrive?

Where do you arrive? (*Wo* kommst du an?)

What do I do? (*Was* tue ich?)

How does the uniform fit him? (*Wie* steht ihm die Uniform?)

Why does she visit Paul? (*Warum* besucht sie Paul?)

Bei *he/she/it* musst du *does* verwenden!

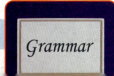

Grammatik

11 Grammar:

Kapitel 9: Die einfache Vergangenheit

Wenn du etwas Vergangenes ausdrücken möchtest, benutzt du das *simple past*. Es gibt nur eine Form für alle Personen.
So gehst du bei den regelmäßigen Tätigkeitswörtern vor.

1. Finde das Tätigkeitswort.
   Emily *visits* Paul at home. (Emily *besucht* Paul zu Hause.)

2. Bilde die Grundform.
   Emily visits ⇒ *to visit* (Emily besucht ⇒ *besuchen*)

3. Setze die Grundform ohne *to* ein und füge *-ed* hinzu.
   Emily *visited* Paul at home. (Emily *besuchte* Paul zu Hause.)

Englisch	Deutsch
I *stay* at home.	Ich *bleibe* zu Hause.
I *stayed* at home.	Ich *blieb* zu Hause.
He *plays* football.	Er *spielt* Fußball.
He *played* football.	Er *spielte* Fußball.

Bei den Tätigkeitswörtern, die in der Grundform auf *-e* enden, wird nur ein *-d* angehängt.

I *arrive* at ten o'clock. (Ich *komme* um zehn Uhr *an*.)

I *arrived* at ten o'clock. (Ich *kam* um zehn Uhr *an*.)

Viele Tätigkeitswörter sind unregelmäßig.
Du musst die Vergangenheitsformen wie Vokabeln lernen.

I *do* my homework. (Ich *mache* meine Hausaufgaben.)

I *did* my homework. (Ich *machte* meine Hausaufgaben.)

I *go* at ten o'clock. (Ich *gehe* um zehn Uhr.)

I *went* at ten o'clock. (Ich *ging* um zehn Uhr.)

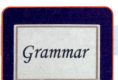

Die Uhrzeit

So gehst du vor, um die Uhrzeit nennen zu können:
Teile die Uhr in zwei Hälften ein.

Die Zeitangaben der ersten halben Stunde (orangefarbene Hälfte) beziehen sich auf die vorherige Stunde: Minute 1 bis Minute 30.

Die Zeitangaben der zweiten halben Stunde (grüne Hälfte) beziehen sich auf die folgende Stunde: Minute 31 bis Minute 60.

Englisch		Deutsch	
It is 1 minute	*past three.*	Es ist 1 Minute	*nach drei.*
It is 5 minutes	*past three.*	Es ist 5 Minuten	*nach drei.*
It is 15 minutes/a quarter	*past three.*	Es ist Viertel	*nach drei.*
It is 20 minutes	*past three.*	Es ist 20 Minuten	*nach drei.*
It is 30 minutes/half	*past three.*	Es ist	*halb vier.*
It is 10 minutes	*to four.*	Es ist zehn Minuten	*vor vier.*
It is 3 minutes	*to four.*	Es ist drei Minuten	*vor vier.*
It is 15 minutes/a quarter	*to four.*	Es ist Viertel	*vor vier.*
It is	*four o'clock.*	Es ist	*vier Uhr.*

Grammatik

Dictionary

A

to act	– aufführen
again	– wieder, noch einmal
an alien	– ein Außerirdischer
angrily	– ärgerlich
an animal	– ein Tier
to answer	– antworten
an apple	– ein Apfel
an argument	– ein Argument
an arm	– ein Arm
to arrange	– arrangieren,
	– herrichten
as much as	– so viel
to ask	– fragen
at	– an, bei auf, in

B

a balcony	– ein Balkon
a balloon	– ein Ballon
a banana	– eine Banane
a bank	– ein Bank
a basket	– ein Korb
basketball	– Basketball
a bathroom	– ein Badezimmer
a bed	– ein Bett
a bedroom	– ein Schlafzimmer
behind	– hinter
a bell	– eine Glocke, eine Klingel
to belong	– gehören
below	– unter, unten
beside	– neben
best	– beste(r)
better	– besser
between	– zwischen
a bicycle	– ein Fahrrad
big	– groß
a bin	– ein Mülleimer
black	– schwarz

blonde	– blond
a blouse	– eine Bluse
blue	– blau
a board	– eine Tafel
a book	– ein Buch
a box	– eine Kiste
(pl. boxes)	– (Kisten)
a boy	– ein Junge
breakdance	– Breakdance
a bridge	– eine Brücke
a broom	– ein Besen
a budgie	– ein Wellensittich
a building	– ein Gebäude
to build	– bauen
a bus	– ein Bus
(pl. busses)	– (Busse)
butter	– Butter
to buy	kaufen

C

a cage	– ein Käfig
a candle	– eine Kerze
a car	– ein Auto
a card	– eine Karte
careful	– vorsichtig
carefully	– sorgfältig
a carpet	– ein Teppich
a carrot	– eine Möhre, eine Karotte
to carry out	– raustragen
a cat	– eine Katze
a category	– eine Kategorie, Rubrik
(pl. categories)	(Kategorien)
a celebration	– eine Feier
a chair	– ein Stuhl
a chant	– ein Gesang
to check	– überprüfen
a child	– ein Kind
(pl. children)	(Kinder)

a chimney	– ein Schornstein
chocolate	– Schokolade
to choose	– auswählen
a Christmas card	– eine Weihnachtskarte
a Christmas tree	– ein Weihnachtsbaum
a cinema	– ein Kino
a city	– eine Stadt
a class	– eine Klasse
a classmate	– ein Mitschüler, eine Mitschülerin
a classroom	– ein Klassenraum
to clean	– putzen
clearly	– klar, deutlich
a clock	– eine Uhr
clothes (pl.)	– Kleidung
a coat	– ein Mantel
to collect	– (ein)sammeln
a colour	– eine Farbe
to colour in	– anmalen
to come	– kommen
to compare	– vergleichen
complicated	– kompliziert
a computer	– ein Computer
to copy	– abschreiben
cornflakes (pl.)	– Cornflakes
correct	– richtig
a couch	– ein Sofa, – eine Couch
to count	– zählen
a country (pl. countries)	– ein Land – (Länder)
a cousin	– ein Cousin, eine Cousine
a cover	– ein Deckblatt
cress	– Kresse
to cross out	– durchstreichen
a cupboard	– ein Schrank
to cut	– schneiden
to cycle	– Fahrrad fahren

D

damp	– feucht
to decide	– entscheiden
to decorate	– dekorieren
to describe	– beschreiben
a desk	– ein Schreibtisch
a detective	– ein Detektiv
a dialogue	– ein Gespräch
a dictionary	– ein Wörterbuch
different	– anders
to discuss	– Diskutieren
a discussion	– eine Diskussion, ein Gespräch
to divide	– teilen
Do not worry!	– Mache dir keine Sorgen!
Do you like …?	– Magst du …?
a dog	– ein Hund
a door	– eine Tür
a dragon	– ein Drache
to draw	– abzeichnen, – zeichnen
a dream	– ein Traum
to dress	– anziehen, kleiden
to drink	– trinken
to drop	– fallen lassen

E

each	– jede, jeder, jedes
an ear	– ein Ohr
an Easter bunny	– ein Osterhase
easy	– leicht, einfach
to eat	– essen
education	– Bildung, Erziehung
an egg	– ein Ei
eight	– acht
eleven	– elf
ever	– jemals

127

Dictionary

everything	– alles		
excited	– aufgeregt		**G**
an exhibition	– eine Ausstellung	a gallery	– eine Galerie
to explain	– erklären	a game	– ein Spiel
an eye	– ein Auge	a gate	– ein Tor
		a ghost	– ein Geist
		a girl	– ein Mädchen
F		to give	– geben
		a glass	– ein Glas
a factory	– eine Fabrik	glue	– Klebstoff
a family	– eine Familie	to go back	– zurückgehen
(pl. families)	– (Familien)	to go forwards	– vorgehen
fat	– dick	to go to	– gehen nach/zu
Father Christmas	– Weihnachtsmann	golf	– Golf
		gone	– verloren
favourite	– Liebling(s)	good	– gut
a fence	– ein Zaun	Good luck!	– Viel Glück!
to find	– finden	Good morning!	– Guten Morgen!
a finger	– ein Finger	grass	– Gras
a fire	– ein Feuer	great	– großartig, toll
first	– zuerst	green	– grün
five	– fünf	a guinea pig	– ein Meerschweinchen
to fix	– befestigen		
to fold	– falten		
a folder	– eine Mappe		
to follow	– folgen	**H**	
food	– Futter, Essen		
a foot (pl. feet)	– ein Fuß (Füße)	hair (pl.)	– Haare
football	– Fußball	a hall	– ein Flur
to forget	– vergessen	a hamburger	– ein Hamburger
to form	– bilden	a hamster	– ein Hamster
four	– vier	a hamster wheel	– ein Laufrad
fourteen	– vierzehn		
fresh	– frisch	a hand	– eine Hand
Friday	– Freitag	to hang	– aufhängen
a friend	– ein Freund, eine Freundin	to happen	– passieren
		a hat	– ein Hut
friendly	– freundlich	to hate	– hassen
from	– aus, von	to have	– haben, besitzen
fun	– Spaß	he	– er
furniture (pl.)	– Möbel	a head	– ein Kopf
		Hello!	– Hallo!

to help	– helfen
here	– hier
a hobby	– ein Hobby
(pl. hobbies)	– (Hobbys)
a hole	– ein Loch
a hotel	– ein Hotel
a house	– ein Haus
how	– wie
How old are you?	– Wie alt bist du?

I/Me	– ich
I am … years old.	– Ich bin … Jahre alt.
an ice-cream	– ein Eis
an idea	– eine Idee
important	– wichtig
in	– in, auf
in front of	– vor
information	– Information
into	– in
an instruction	– eine Anweisung
an interview partner	– ein Interview-partner
to introduce someone/ something	– jemanden/ etwas vorstellen

a jacket	– eine Jacke
to do judo	– Judo (machen)

ketchup	– Ketchup
a kitchen	– eine Küche
a knee	– ein Knie
to know	– kennen, wissen

L

a language	– eine Sprache
a lantern	– eine Laterne
late	– spät
later	– später
to lead	– führen, leiten
to learn	– lernen
a leg	– ein Bein
a letter	– ein Brief
like	– ähnlich wie
to like	– mögen, gern haben
a list	– eine Liste
to listen	– (zu)hören
a little bit	– ein bisschen
to live	– leben
a living room	– ein Wohnzimmer
long	– lang
a long time ago	– vor langer Zeit
to look at	– ansehen
to look for someone/ something	– jemanden/ etwas suchen
to look up	– nachschauen, nachschlagen
a lot of	– viel(e)
loudly	– laut
to love	– lieben

to make	– machen
a map	– eine Karte
to mark	– beschriften
May I ask you some questions?	– Darf ich dir/Ihnen/ euch ein paar Fragen stellen?
maybe	– vielleicht
means of transportation	– Transportmittel

129

Dictionary

to meet	– treffen	notes (pl.)	– Notizen
milk	– Milch	a number	– eine Zahl
a mirror cabinet	– ein Spiegelkabinett		
to miss a turn	– (eine Runde) aussetzen	**O**	
missing	– weg	an object	– ein Gegenstand
a mistletoe	– ein Mistelzweig	old	– alt
mixed up	– durcheinander	on, onto	– an, auf, in
Monday	– Montag	one	– eins
a monster	– ein Monster	to open	– öffnen
a motorcycle	– ein Motorrad	other	– anderer, andere, anderes
a mountain bike	– ein Mountainbike		
a mouse (pl. mice)	– eine Maus (Mäuse)	**P**	
a mouth	– ein Mund		
to move in	– einziehen, umziehen	a page	– eine Seite
music	– Musik	to paint something	– etwas anstreichen
must	– müssen	a pair of jeans	– eine Jeans
my	– mein, meine	a pair of shoes	– ein Paar Schuhe
		a pair of shorts	– eine kurze Hose, Shorts
		a pair of socks	– ein Paar Socken
		a pair of trousers	– eine (lange) Hose
N		parents (pl.)	– Eltern
a name	– ein Name	a park	– ein Park
to name	– bezeichnen, benennen	a part of the body	– ein Körperteil
necessary	– nötig, notwendig	a party (pl. parties)	– eine Party (Partys)
a necessity	– Notwendigkeit	a peanut	– eine Erdnuss
to need	– brauchen	a pen	– ein Füller
a neighbour	– ein Nachbar	a pencil	– ein Bleistift
new	– neu	a pencil-case	– eine Federmappe
nice	– hübsch, nett, schön	people (pl.)	– Leute, Menschen
a night	– eine Nacht	a pet	– ein Haustier
nine	– neun	a photo	– ein Foto
a nose	– eine Nase	a picture	– ein Bild
not	– nicht	pink	– rosa
a note	– eine Note, Notiz		

a pirate	– ein Pirat	to ride a horse	– ein Pferd reiten
a place	– ein Platz	to roll the dice	– würfeln
a planet	– ein Planet	rollerblades (pl.)	– Rollschuhe
to play	– spielen		
to point at something	– auf etwas zeigen	a roof	– ein Dach
possible	– möglich	a room	– ein Raum, ein Zimmer
a poster	– ein Poster	a rubber	– ein Radiergummi
to prepare	– vorbereiten	a ruler	– ein Lineal
to present	– präsentieren, zeigen	to run	– laufen, rennen
a present	– ein Geschenk		
a pumpkin	– ein Kürbis		
to punch	– lochen, stanzen		
a pupil	– eine Schülerin, ein Schüler		

S

a pupils' magazine	– eine Schülerzeitschrift
to push	– schieben, drücken
to put	– legen, setzen, stellen

a sandwich	– ein Sandwich
Saturday	– Samstag
to say	– sagen
to say something to someone	– jemandem etwas sagen
a school	– eine Schule
a school uniform	– eine Schuluniform
a schoolbag	– eine Schultasche
science	– Wissenschaft
scissors (pl.)	– eine Schere
to see	– sehen
a sentence	– ein Satz
seven	– sieben
a sharpener	– ein Anspitzer
she	– sie
a sheet of paper	– ein Blatt Papier
a shirt	– ein Oberhemd
a shoe	– ein Schuh
to shop	– einkaufen
a shop	– ein Geschäft
short	– kurz
a shoulder	– eine Schulter
to show	– zeigen
a sign	– ein Schild, ein Zeichen

Q

a question	– eine Frage

R

a rabbit	– ein Kaninchen
to read	– lesen
a reader	– ein Leser
red	– rot
a relative	– eine Verwandte, ein Verwandter
a renovation week	– eine Renovierungswoche
to repeat	– wiederholen
a restaurant	– ein Restaurant
a result	– ein Ergebnis
a rhyme	– ein Reim
a riddle	– ein Rätsel

Dictionary

to sing	– singen			
six	– sechs	**T**		
a skateboard	– ein Skateboard	a table	– ein Tisch	
a skeleton	– ein Skelett		hier: eine Tabelle	
a skirt	– ein Rock	table tennis	– Tischtennis	
to sleep	– schlafen	to take	– nehmen	
a sleigh	– ein Schlitten	tall	– groß (Körpergröße)	
slowly	– langsam	a taxi	– ein Taxi	
small	– klein	a teacher	– eine Lehrerin,	
sometimes	– manchmal		ein Lehrer	
a song	– das Lied	a television	– ein Fernseher	
to sound	– klingen	to tell	– erzählen	
to speak	– sprechen	ten	– zehn	
special	– besonders	tennis	– Tennis	
a spider	– eine Spinne	Thank you.	– Danke.	
sports (pl.)	– Sport	the world	– die Welt	
to spread	– verteilen	a theatre	– ein Theater	
squash	– Squash	their	– ihr, ihre	
to stand up	– aufstehen	thin	– dünn	
to start	– anfangen, beginnen	a thing	– eine Sache	
to stay	– bleiben	to think about	– denken,	
a steak	– ein Steak		nachdenken	
to stick	– stecken	thirteen	– dreizehn	
a stocking	– ein Strumpf	this	– dies, dieser, diese,	
a stone	– ein Stein		dieses	
a strategy	– eine Strategie	three	– drei	
a street	– eine Straße	to throw	– werfen	
a street map	– eine Straßenkarte	Thursday	– Donnerstag	
streetball	– Streetball	a timetable	– ein Stundenplan	
a streetlamp	– eine Straßenlaterne	a tissue	– ein Taschentuch	
a string	– ein Bindfaden	a title	– ein Titel	
a subject	– ein Thema,	a toast	– ein Toast	
	ein Unterrichtsfach	today	– heute	
Sunday	– Sonntag	a toe	– ein Zeh	
a supermarket	– ein Supermarkt	too	– auch, zu	
a sweatshirt	– ein Sweatshirt	to touch	– berühren, anfassen	
sweets (pl.)	– Süßigkeiten	a town	– eine Stadt	
to swim	– schwimmen	a toy mouse	– eine Spielzeugmaus	
a swimming pool	– ein Schwimmbad	a tram	– eine Straßenbahn	
		to travel	– reisen	
		a treat	– eine Leckerei	
		a trick	– ein Streich	

to try	– versuchen	to whisper	– flüstern
a T-shirt	– ein T-Shirt	white	– weiß
the tube	– die (Londoner) U-Bahn	why	– warum
		to win	– gewinnen
a tube	– ein Rohr, eine Tube	a window	– ein Fenster
Tuesday	– Dienstag	a witch	– eine Hexe
a turn	– eine Runde	(pl. witches)	– (Hexen)
twelve	– zwölf	with	– mit
two	– zwei	wood	– Holz
		wooden	– hölzern, aus Holz
		a word	– ein Wort
		a work	– eine Arbeit
		to write	– schreiben
U		to write back	– zurückschreiben, antworten
under	– unter, unten		
to use	– nutzen	to write down	– aufschreiben

V		**Y**	
a vampire	– ein Vampir	a year	– ein Jahr
very	– sehr	yellow	– gelb
a video	– ein Video	yours	– dein(e), euer, Ihr
to visit	– besuchen	yourself	– dich, selber, selbst

W		**Z**	
a wall	– eine Wand	a zebra	– ein Zebra
to want	– wollen	a zoo	– ein Zoo
a wardrobe	– ein Kleiderschrank		
to watch television (TV)	– fernsehen		
water	– Wasser		
to water	– bewässern, gießen		
a way	– ein Weg, eine Methode		
to wear	– (Kleidung) tragen		
Wednesday	– Mittwoch		
well-organised	– gut organisiert		
what	– was, wie, welche/r/s		
What is your name?	– Wie heißt du?		

In English, please!

Beginn und Ende

Good morning.	Guten Morgen.
How are you?	Wie geht es dir/euch/Ihnen?
I am fine.	Mir geht es gut.
Good bye.	Auf Wiedersehen.
See you tomorrow.	Bis morgen.

Fragen

I have got a question.	Ich habe eine Frage.
Can anyone help me?	Kann mir jemand helfen?
Maybe I can help you.	Vielleicht kann ich dir helfen.
I do not understand that.	Ich verstehe das nicht.
Could you say that again?	Kannst du/Können Sie das wiederholen?
What is "Schultasche" in English?	Was heißt „Schultasche" auf Englisch?
What is "schoolbag" in German?	Was heißt „schoolbag" auf Deutsch?
May I borrow your ruler?	Darf ich mir dein Lineal ausleihen?
Thank you/Thanks!	Danke!
May I go to the toilet, please?	Darf ich zur Toilette gehen?
May I open the window, please?	Darf ich das Fenster öffnen?

Arbeitsanweisungen

Work with your neighbour.	Arbeitet mit eurem Nachbarn. Arbeite mit deinem Nachbarn.
Open your books on page … please.	Schlagt bitte euer Buch auf Seite … auf.
Come and sit in a circle.	Kommt her und macht einen Sitzkreis.
Form two teams, please.	Bildet bitte zwei Teams.
All together now!	Und nun alle zusammen!
Let us play/sing …	Lasst uns spielen/singen …
Are you ready?	Seid ihr bereit?

Lob und Ermahnung

That is right.	Das ist richtig.
Well done!	Gut gemacht!
Attention, please.	Ich bitte um Aufmerksamkeit.
Could you be quiet, please!	Bitte seid leise!

Entschuldigung

Sorry, I am late.	Entschuldigen Sie die Verspätung.
Sorry, I do not have my exercise book/my homework.	Entschuldigung, ich habe mein Heft/meine Hausaufgaben nicht.

Bildnachweis: © Destination Bristol: S. 77 – Inga Ettelt, Hannover: S. 18/19, 20, 49, 58/59 – Anke Heiser, Bonn: S. 96 – Karin Möcklinghoff, Hamburg: S. 26 – MEV Verlags GmbH, Augsburg: S. 6/7, 78 – J. Moser, Amberg: S. 38 – Kevin Patterson, Hannover: S. 88, 104 – picture alliance: 64, 78, 92/93 – Claudia Riedel, Bonn: S. 47 – Schapowalow/Fahn: S. 84 – M.Venus, Regensburg: S. 78; Witch, Witch © A. Druce 1991. Reproduced by permission of Child`s Play (International) Ltd. All rights reserved: S. 94

Grafik: Raimo Bergt, Berlin

Technische Grafik: Elisabeth Galas, Köln

Umschlaggestaltung: Astrid Sitz, Köln